KENNETH

G000127542

SIEGE MINES AND UNDERGROUND WARFARE

SHIRE ARCHAEOLOGY

Cover illustration:
Detail from a cutaway model of a mine approaching the eastern curtain wall of King John's
Castle, Limerick, during the siege of 1642, based on archaeological excavations at the
castle in 1990. The model is on permanent display at the King John's Castle visitor centre.
(Photograph by Miguel Müller)

British Library Cataloguing in Publication data:
Wiggins, Kenneth
Siege mines and underground warfare. – (Shire archaeology; 84)
1. Siege warfare – History
2. Mines (Military explosives)
3. Mining engineering
4. Tunnel warfare – History
I. Title
355.4'4'09
ISBN 0 7478 0547 4.

Published in 2003 by
SHIRE PUBLICATIONS LTD
Cromwell House, Church Street, Princes Risborough,
Buckinghamshire HP27 9AA, UK.
(Website: www.shirebooks.co.uk)

Series Editor: James Dyer.

Number 84 in the Shire Archaeology series.

ISBN 0 7478 0547 4.

First published 2003.

Printed in Great Britain by
CIT Printing Services Ltd, Press Buildings,
Merlins Bridge, Haverfordwest, Pembrokeshire SA61 1XF.

Contents

Acknowledgements

My thanks go to John Rotheroe at Shire for his decision to commission this book, and also to James Dyer, Series Editor, for reading the typescript and making many useful comments. I am very grateful to Sarah Hodder, Design Editor, for her efforts in guiding the work through to publication. The assistance provided by Piet Chielens, Co-ordinator, In Flanders Fields Museum, Ypres, in obtaining the photographs of the Spanbroekmolen crater is greatly appreciated. My deepest thanks, as ever, go to my wife, Eileen, who came up with the initial idea, and who made sure I stuck to the task until it was finished.

List of illustrations

1
Introduction

Siege warfare, the attack and defence of fortified places, has been a feature of human conflict since the dawn of history. The greatest sieges of the past have an epic quality about them, and many tales of courage, suffering and endurance continue to live on long after the participants themselves have passed away. Stories from sieges that still inform the popular imagination include, for example, the legend of the wooden horse of Troy, which tells of how an immensely protracted siege was brought to a sudden conclusion by a bold and ingenious stroke of invention.

Open military combat on the field of battle is bloody and intense, but until the nineteenth century the result was decided relatively quickly, often in the space of a single day. The great land battles of history were engagements between armed and trained soldiery, whereas sieges could involve whole communities, including women and children. This factor contributes to the image of siege warfare as more harrowing and poignant than open combat. Sieges could be just as decisive as encounters on the battlefield, but their very nature meant that the action unfolded over a much longer time span and many different stratagems could be adopted by the attacking side before a castle or walled town was reduced. Sieges were frequently as much a test of endurance for the besiegers as they were for the besieged, and the demands made by the prolonged attempt to capture a vital stronghold could grind down the attacking side more rapidly than they could a well-provisioned garrison maintaining a stubborn resistance.

There were many options available to an army that elected to encamp before the fortified seat of an opposing power. The ramparts that provided the main line of defence for the besieged were probably stout and well manned, and were likely to be supplemented with external ditches or natural features that made the work of direct approach both difficult and dangerous. Assault by main force would be hazardous and costly in human life if a breach or breaches were not first made in the outer defences, giving the attacking units an opening upon which to concentrate their efforts with at least some chance of gaining access to the inner line of defences. Throughout history the quest for artillery capable of smashing the strongest walls was a fundamental challenge that military technology attempted to address, resulting in the construction of the great stone-throwing engines of the pre-gunpowder age, and subsequently in the design of heavy cannon that could discharge solid stone or metal shot of enormous size.

However, there was available to the armed forces contemplating the taking of an enemy fortification another means of breaching the ramparts that sheltered the opposition and prevented the two sides from engaging directly with each other. Every wall has a foundation and, if that foundation is removed by undermining or 'sapping', the wall itself will sink, split, shatter or collapse, depending on how the work is carried out. Digging was an alternative way of opening up the defences of a fortified site to make possible a frontal assault, and this method did not rely on an array of large and expensive wall-breaking artillery.

The undermining of walls at some point in the course of a siege was not a simple matter, nor could it be undertaken without considerable risk to the individuals contemplating such work. There can be no doubt, because undermining could be attempted with a basic range of hand tools, that it must belong to the earliest and most primitive forms of siege warfare. But the development and use of heavy artillery never at any point superseded digging, and at all periods of history, including the twentieth century, the pick and the shovel continued to have an important role to play in military affairs.

The practice of digging under the walls of a citadel or some other defended structure was a skilled business that was best left to individuals with training and experience in working underground. The specialists in this area were those men who made a living from mines in which metal ores or other minerals were excavated via shafts and tunnels for commercial purposes, often at depths far below the surface. Miners had expertise in the digging and shoring of tunnels that other civilians could not match, and it is a feature of siege warfare through the ages that the undermining of defences was invariably attempted by men who were already miners by trade. The techniques of siege mining had much in common with conventional mining, but with quite different objectives. The aim in mineral working was to extract as much as possible of any valuable natural resources that could be found in an underground seam, while at all times avoiding damage to the galleries in which the miners laboured. In contrast, the purpose of siege mining was the 'springing' · of the end of a gallery by burning the timber props that supported it, or by packing it with gunpowder to cause an explosion, in order to destroy as much as possible of the structure under which the mine had been brought. Therefore, destruction, albeit planned and deliberate in nature, was the objective of the miner answering the call in time of war, although tunnelling could also be used to gain entry to a fortification under cover of darkness, allowing a surprise attack to be made on the unsuspecting garrison.

If the digging of subterranean tunnels was not possible, undermining could be commenced at ground level at the foot of the wall that was to be brought down. This type of 'sapping' had the disadvantage of taking place in full view of the garrison, and the miners had to be protected

·

1. A medieval representation of covered mining during a siege. The diggers, armed with picks, busily work under the protection of a wheeled mantlet made of timber and hides, while the men on the parapet do their best to break it up. (Peter Newark's Military Pictures)

from showers of missiles launched by the defenders above them by a portable cover or 'mantlet' (figure 1). If their protection was strong enough to withstand the best efforts of the garrison to destroy it, the sappers could pick out stones at the base of the wall and establish props below the masonry that could be burned down to achieve an effective collapse of part of the structure.

Gallery mining was a more effective option as it had the advantage of being commenced at a point some distance from the object wall and was not visible to the defenders as the approach was by means of a tunnel driven well below ground level. It was much more of a concern for the defenders, who had to devise some means of establishing the direction the mines were coming from, and at what depth. To intercept and deflect the serious threat posed by gallery mining, the garrison had little choice but to meet the approaching menace with underground works of its own, known as countermines. Sieges at which mining and countermining were carried out by the participants could be remarkable, frequently resulting in hand-to-hand combat when opposing tunnels

2. Woodcut from a sixteenth-century military text showing miners driving a gallery mine towards the angle bastion of a walled town. There is plenty of activity with picks, shovels and wheelbarrows, and enough headroom to stand upright, but no evidence for the use of timber props to support the structure. (From Leonhard Fronsperger, *Kriegsbuch*, III [1573, f. CLXVIv]. By courtesy of the Newberry Library, Chicago)

broke into each other, and the outcome of a particular siege could be determined by events played out far below the surface (figure 2).

Variations on the theme of siege mining were practised in every century in history, and from the moment it first became apparent that even the strongest wall was vulnerable to unseen attack from miners burrowing somewhere deep in the earth, the threat of mining exercised a fundamental influence on the evolution of military architecture. Because mining took place underground, the potential for activity of this type to be preserved as evidence uncovered during the archaeological excavation of walled towns and castles is considerable. The use of tunnelling as an important aspect of the attack and defence of places was something that first came to be considered by a number of ancient authorities, and much has been written about it by experts since the medieval period. This short account looks at the course of siege mining from the earliest times, outlining its origins and development through the ages, its impact on fortress warfare and on the design of fortifications, and its treatment in military literature, as well as the potential that archaeological excavation has in shedding more light on the nature of this fascinating subject.

2
Antiquity

The ancient origins of siege attack by mining can be traced through archaeology as far back as the period 883–859 BC. An orthostat relief found at the palace of Ashurnasirpal II at Nimrud in Assyria depicts several methods of assault taking place during a siege, and several figures are shown at work underneath the walls of a stronghold (figure 3). However, the business of reducing a fortification most commonly involved storming attacks with ladders, and the construction of engines of various types, and these devices were to endure well beyond the demise of the ancient civilisations.

Some classical writers tried to take a scientific look at the topic of siege warfare, and their works, in translations and new editions, were hugely influential into the medieval and early modern periods. The Greek historian Aeneas Tacticus, writing a practical work in the fourth century BC entitled *How to Survive under Siege*, was notable for his detailed discussion of the subject.

The Roman authority Vitruvius, writing in the first century AD, described the main engines that were constructed for sieges. Broadly speaking, there were four distinct types: the throwing engines, for example catapults and *ballistae* (giant crossbows); movable towers, allowing besiegers to ascend and cross on to the enemy's parapet;

3. Part of the upper band of a carved orthostat from the palace of Ashurnasirpal II at Nimrud, Assyria, dating from the ninth century BC, representing the siege of a city, drawn by A. H. Layard in 1849. At the bottom right-hand corner, a miner is shown burrowing his way underneath the base of a wall. (© Copyright The British Museum)

4. Classical siege warfare seen through eighteenth-century eyes. The countermine gallery, extending from the courtyard on the right-hand side, has been taken well outside the garrison's wall and below its own ditch in order to burn the props, the intention being to collapse the enemy's siege tower. A mine driven by the besiegers, at the extreme left-hand side, is converging rapidly on the head of the countermine. Illustration by Chevalier Follard from a French edition of Polybius's history of Rome, published in 1727. (The Mansell Collection. By courtesy of Rex Features Limited)

demolition weapons, for example the ram and the borer; and engines to protect men picking at the base of a wall. In terms of undermining, Vitruvius refers to two distinct forms: ground-level or covered mining, and underground or gallery mining. Ground-level mining took place under movable timber covers, fitted with oxhides, known as 'tortoises'. These could be smashed by dropping missiles or set alight by blazing arrows from above. The tortoise or *testudo* could also be adapted to house a battering ram, fitted with a hardened iron head, or a borer, differing from the ram by having a sharp iron tip to gouge at the masonry. Digging at the base of a wall could also be commenced on the lower level of tall movable siege towers once the ditch had been infilled and the tower was pushed up into position. Gallery mining could be undertaken to achieve different ends. First, the mine could be brought up into the interior of the fortress or walled town at a secret point, allowing the attacking soldiers to issue from it and take the garrison unawares. Such a mine was made by the Romans during the epic siege of the town of Veii, which lasted several years until the town fell in 396

BC. Second, the miners, having dug below the foundations, propped the mine-head with timbers, which were set on fire to collapse and wreck the masonry. Burnt-prop mining was used at the Carthaginian siege of Himera on Sicily in 412 BC. Countermine galleries excavated by the garrison could also be advanced beyond the walls to wreck the works of the surrounding army, creating destructive subsidence once the props were burnt (figure 4). Hand-to-hand combat in a breakthrough between a mine and a countermine is described by the historian Livy at the siege of the Greek city of Ambracia in 189 BC. The counterminers used smoke to drive the Romans from their mine.

In terms of the breadth of his approach and the extraordinary influence of his work, the later Roman writer Flavius Vegetius Renatus, the author of *Epitoma Rei Militaris*, dating from AD 388–92, was the most significant classical authority on military affairs. An important English translation by John Sadler appeared as *The Foure Books of Martiall Policye* in 1572. Vegetius is relatively thorough in his treatment of siege engines, and the practice of covered mining under fabricated shelters is touched upon, as is the digging of the underground mine. He notes that in the Roman army the prefect of engineers had duties that included responsibility for the sapping of walls by underpinned mines. He stresses that one of the best defences against subterranean works was the digging of as wide and deep a ditch as possible around a town, as mines could be prevented 'by the depth and by the flooding of fosses'.

The ancient sources for siege warfare reveal familiarity with the various manoeuvres and strategies that could be brought into play in the course of a siege. Sapping the foundations of a wall was one of the available options, and the routine of constructing covers or 'mantlets' to accommodate workmen armed with picks, or the opening of underground galleries, would have been understood by military commanders and their engineering subordinates. However, the writers in general, while aware of the practice of gallery mining, never consider in detail how such tunnels were made or what they looked like, and we find little technical elaboration on the subject.

3
The medieval period

The authorities for siege warfare in the post-Roman centuries describe the use of battering rams, stone-throwing engines and siege towers ('belfries'). A deadly new invention, 'Greek fire', an inflammable oil-based formula that exploded on impact when expelled from specially made siphons, was significant in the defence of Constantinople (674–8). It may be assumed that the strength of many a foundation was tested by pickaxe during numerous early medieval sieges, but we do not hear much about mining of any kind until the ninth century. There are references to mining at the siege of Barcelona around 800 and at Bergamo in 894. In most cases, the undermining of walls is usually an indication of covered sapping rather than the digging of long galleries. Covered mining activity is recorded at the siege of Chester in 918. On this occasion, the wicker hurdles protecting the diggers were reinforced to resist boulders cast down from the ramparts, but in the end the garrison beat off the attackers by the novel expedient of pitching beehives into their midst! We hear very little of gallery mining at this stage in history. The best-documented siege of the early medieval period was the Viking attack on Paris in 885. This siege was notable for featuring, in the words of historian Charles Oman, practically 'every device of siegecraft' that was known at the time. Covered mining underneath a mantlet was tried out, but the work was disrupted when the mantlets were wrecked by fire. However, the Vikings appear to have responded by driving underground a gallery mine, which was set alight and so created a breach, although the subsequent assault was a failure.

The mature medieval age between the eleventh and fourteenth centuries brought the rise and consolidation of feudal Europe, and with it the proliferation of castles and improvements to urban defences. The siting and design of castles reflected concerns about mining, and military architects were anxious to devise works that eliminated this threat. Round angle towers and keeps came to replace square or rectangular plans, as these were thought to offer better protection from mining. Building prominently on elevated solid rock outcrops was considered to be very secure, but the provision of a broad wet ditch was regarded as the best deterrent to this form of attack (figure 5). Sieges were a regular feature of the period but, broadly speaking, there was no fundamental change in the tactics adopted by besieging armies. The role of the mine in breaching strongly defended walls was still recognised, but by the later twelfth century a major new engine had emerged, which brought

5. Building on rock was a strong deterrent to the pick and shovel, but water provided the only absolute guarantee of protection from mining. The purpose behind wet defences was to make a castle as mine-proof as possible, and at Caerphilly Castle in Glamorgan we see this thinking taken to its limits. (Photograph: Cadbury Lamb)

with it an improved wall-breaking capability. This was the counterweight trebuchet, the foremost artillery weapon of the pre-gunpowder era.

Britain

In Britain, mining appears early on in the Norman conquest, at William the Conqueror's siege of Exeter in 1067. The anarchy that accompanied the reign of Stephen (1135–54) involved considerable siege activity. Stephen summoned men who were skilled in mining underground to dig tunnels to demolish the walls of Exeter in 1136. However, the mining effort was not instrumental in ending the siege; only when the wells in the castle dried out did the garrison feel compelled to surrender. At the siege of Lincoln in 1143, eighty workmen suffocated in trenches dug during the mining of the castle. A mine gallery 7.3 metres long was revealed during excavations by Hugh Braun in 1935 at Bungay Castle, Suffolk. The excavator dated the work to the capture of the castle by Henry II in 1174. The mine had two lateral galleries, giving the complete work a cruciform plan (figure 6). The interior of the forebuilding along the southern side of the keep was excavated, exposing one end of the mine and allowing access underneath the keep's south-western corner (figure 7).

Three of the most significant sieges in Britain in this period occurred in the early thirteenth century, and mining played a vital role in each. The siege at Rochester Castle, Kent, in 1215 is one of the best-known instances of the use of mining in castle warfare in the medieval period. The siege was directed in person by King John, beginning on 11th October 1215. When bombardment of the castle failed to produce any

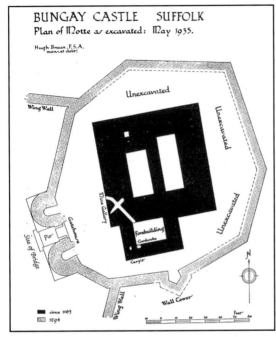

6. Plan of Bungay Castle, Suffolk, showing the cruciform mine gallery, as excavated in 1935, extending between the north-west angle of the forebuilding and the south-west angle of the keep. (By permission of the Suffolk Institute of Archaeology and History)

7. View of the entrance to the mine gallery at the south-west angle of the excavated forebuilding at Bungay Castle, Suffolk. The excavator believed the mine dated from the surrender of the castle to Henry II in 1174. (By permission of the Suffolk Institute of Archaeology and History)

effect, miners were called in, with the result that part of the bailey wall collapsed. The garrison withdrew to the keep, and after another unsuccessful assault the 'underwallers' were set to work again, leading to the destruction of a corner of the keep. The mine was fired with combustibles, including the fat of forty bacon pigs! Remarkably, the stubborn garrison retreated behind a cross-wall in the keep and held out for a while longer. The final surrender came after a resistance of nearly two months. The effectiveness of a team of miners in the absence of other means of breaking down walls was never more ably demonstrated. The keep was subsequently repaired with a round angle tower at the south-eastern corner, which contrasts with the original square towers at the other corners (figure 8).

The siege of Dover Castle, Kent, by Prince Louis of France commenced in June 1216. Stone-throwing engines and a battering ram were brought

8. View of the keep at Rochester Castle, Kent. The original square corner towers contrast with the round south-eastern corner tower, which was reconstructed in a more mine-resistant style following the demolition of this angle by miners during the siege of 1215. (© English Heritage. NMR)

9. A chalk-cut tunnel at Dover Castle, Kent, which may date from the siege of 1216. (Photograph: Peter Chèze-Brown from Charles Kightly, *Stronghold of the Realm*, Thames & Hudson, 1979)

into action, but one of the towers of the gatehouse was brought down by a mine. The French were unable to storm the breach, and a truce was called in October 1216 on the news of King John's death. A gallery dug through the solid chalk during this siege still survives (figure 9).

The castle at Bedford was placed under siege between 22nd June and 15th August 1224, during the early part of the reign of Henry III. The siege is notable for being particularly well documented with regard to mining works, and the numerous miners involved came from as far as the Forest of Dean near Gloucester. Bombardment by siege engines was a feature of the operation, but the final assault on the old tower was brought to a conclusion by mining, which caused devastating damage. This was an example of covered mining, as the sappers worked under a mantlet nicknamed the 'cat'. All but the motte of the castle was levelled following the siege.

In general, the British evidence of the period reveals that miners were never called upon to dig at the opening stages of a formal siege. Invariably, in the course of a conventional siege, the mettle of the garrison would be tested by threats and bargaining, leading to battery by engines, and direct assault. Only when other means had failed would recourse to the dangerous practice of mining be contemplated. Miners would be present either as a distinct number in the expeditionary force, or else having been called upon at short notice from the nearest mining district to assist in the siege. So long as the nature of the castle's defences and the quality of the ground permitted the digging of tunnels, there was no doubt that mining could bring about immense destruction. Once the miner was brought into the action, the chances of the garrison successfully facing down the besiegers were greatly diminished.

Continental Europe
The history of siege warfare in Europe in the period 1000–1400 includes many well-documented sieges that provide more evidence for the use of mining in the conquest of towns and castles. The siege of Lisbon in 1147 lasted seventeen weeks and involved considerable technical effort and tactical variation on the part of the besiegers. Movable siege towers were constructed, and a type of stone-throwing weapon known as the 'Balearic mangonel', probably some kind of counterweight engine, was operated during the siege. Covered mining is indicated by reference to a mantlet called a 'sow', and there were some very elaborate gallery mine works also. Unfortunately for the besiegers, a breach caused by mining could not be stormed, and mining played no further part in the course of the siege.

The thirteenth-century evidence for mining at sieges is particularly strong. The prolonged siege in 1203–4 of the immense castle of Château-Gaillard in France, felt at the time to be siege-proof, was largely brought to an end by the efforts of the miners. The outer ward was breached when miners under cover of mantlets picked out the foundations and inserted props, which were then burned to open a breach above. The French went on to gain the middle ward by the unlikely route of scrambling into a garderobe. To take the inner ward, the miners again went to work and, by chance, a rock bridge across the ditch sheltered them as they quarried beneath the foundations. A countermine started by the garrison served only to weaken the structure further. Sustained battering by a large siege engine called a *cabulus*, probably a type of trebuchet, eventually opened a breach, leading to the surrender of the castle.

Siege warfare was a dominant feature of the Hundred Years' War between 1337 and 1453. During this time the technology of sieges was transformed by the introduction and development of the gunpowder cannon as the main instrument of castle warfare. However, in the early fifteenth century the gunpowder revolution had yet to make a difference to the use of mines during sieges. Henry V of England prepared himself for a considerable amount of siege work as he assembled his expedition to France in 1415. His muster of men and equipment included miners. Mining and countermining occurred at Harfleur that year, at Caen in 1417, when the garrison used vibrations on bowls of water to help detect the English mines, and at Melun in 1420. The last was somewhat unusual, as the sources relate that the mine here was used for the purpose of staging 'challenges' between knights of both sides, equipped with sword or battleaxe. Henry himself allegedly took part in one of these individual combats. However, it is very likely that the reality of the wet and muddy conditions in the mines precluded such bouts of chivalrous ritual.

The Crusades

The conduct of sieges beyond the limits of Europe did not differ to any great extent from the experience of warfare in the West, but mining was tactically even more significant. Nikephoros Ouranos, writing *c*.1010, regarded mining as the most effective means for the breaching of walls.

Stone-throwing engines and siege towers were prominently used in these sieges. Covered mining was established during the First Crusade at the close of the eleventh century. Mining underneath a Roman-style *testudo* took place at the siege of Nicaea in 1097, when a tower was collapsed by the firing of beams. Undermining from the ground level of a great siege tower featured at the siege of Marrah the following year. At Jerusalem in 1099, miners worked below a 'sow' and were showered with stones from above, but the crusaders were able to mount the ramparts from a movable tower. Perhaps the greatest of all crusader sieges was that of Acre in 1191, during the Third Crusade. The mining attempted here was not successful.

On the other side, the Muslims were equally adept and were superior to the Europeans in the business of mining, a distinction that Eastern armies were to hold for several centuries. Muslim sources provide a considerable body of evidence on the subject of mining. A remarkable description of what the inside of a siege tunnel looked like is provided by Usamah ibn Munqidh, who made an inspection of one during the siege of Kafartab in 1115 and was most impressed by the quality of the work. He found the gallery to be very narrow, and framed with timber uprights and planks stretched between them to prevent the tunnel collapsing. At the siege of Marqab in 1285, the Knights of St John were under pressure from the relentless progress of the Egyptian miners. When a gallery had been driven below the great tower, the garrison's

10. View of the remains of a tower on the east wall of the ancient stronghold of Ascalon in Israel, built in 1192, incorporating circular through-columns, which made the masonry more cohesive in the event of attack by mining. (From Christopher Marshall, *Warfare in the Latin East, 1192–1291*, 1992. Reproduced by permission of Cambridge University Press)

engineers were invited to survey the works to see the drastic consequences that could follow the firing of the mine. The engineers reported to the governor that their cause was hopeless, and surrender was made with no further action.

Some surviving architectural evidence in crusader lands shows how the threat of mining influenced the construction of fortifications. The twelfth-century castle at Giblet, due north of Beirut in Lebanon, incorporated antique round columns laid transversely through the wall to help reduce the effects of mining. This type of design feature also occurs at the walled city of Ascalon in Israel (figure 10).

4
The explosive mine

The first signs pointing to the potential of gunpowder to influence dramatically the effects of mining during sieges appeared in the fifteenth century. It is possible that an explosive mine, that is, a gallery in which the mine-head was blown up by gunpowder rather than merely burnt down, was used at Orense in Spain in 1468. A failed explosion occurred at Sarzanello in Italy in 1487. However, the most likely candidate for the first fully realised explosive mine is held to be the one exploded at Castel Nuovo (New Castle) in Naples on 27th November 1495. The engineer credited with this success is Francesco di Giorgio Martini. Another important innovator in this field was Pedro Navarro. He directed an explosive mine at San Giorgio in Cephalonia in 1500, and in 1503 exploded a mine under the same Castel Nuovo in Naples that had been mined eight years before. He made others at Castel dell'Ovo (Egg Castle) during the same siege.

The impact of the devastation inflicted by the mines at Naples in 1503 was far reaching. The destructive capabilities of the traditional 'burnt-prop' mine paled in comparison to what a gallery packed with explosives might accomplish. Rumours of the new weapon, followed by practical demonstrations of its awesome power, placed fear of mining uppermost in the continuing evolution of fortifications and defensive strategies.

Military literature in the sixteenth century, emanating in particular from Italian authorities, increasingly wrestled with the problems of attack and defence in an age when the arrival of the siege cannon and new devices such as the explosive mine made accepted theories of warfare look outdated. Because of the increased dangers in mining a wall for the purpose of laying an explosive charge, it was essential that the miner knew exactly what he was doing and had some knowledge of dealing with such problems as how to maximise the damage to the undermined fortification while minimising the risk to his own life. At first there was a certain amount of professional reticence on the subject – a reluctance to reveal too many secrets of the underground terror. The mystery shrouding the new technology is typified by a letter written in 1482 by Leonardo da Vinci, who claimed to know a method for the making of 'secret and tortuous mines'. But eventually military experts came around to discuss at length the techniques of the dangerous business of mining, and, in the sixteenth century, military manuals were produced that attempted to explain how a mine could be constructed and be guaranteed to explode in a controlled way.

An engineer named Mariano di Jacopo, or Il Taccola, had some

21

11. Copy of a late-fifteenth-century drawing by Francesco di Giorgio Martini illustrating the setting of an explosive mine below a mountain citadel. (Reproduced from Bertrand Gille, *The Renaissance Engineers*, 1966. By kind permission of Lund Humphries)

knowledge of the subject when he wrote *De Machinis* in 1449. A far more significant contribution was made by Francesco di Giorgio Martini, also credited with devising the mine at Naples in 1495. His manuscript *Trattati*, composed between 1475 and 1492, contained several drawings of mines and their powder charges (figure 11). The illustrated mines had either curved or zigzagged plans. These bending tunnels (*sinuosi cuniculi*) were to help prevent the explosive force of the gunpowder placed in the chamber at the end of the mine from travelling back along the length of the gallery. The first printed account of gunpowder mining appeared in a book called *Il Vallo*, by Battista della Valle, published in

12. Plan of an explosive mine by Vannoccio Biringuccio from his work *De la Pirotechnia* (f. 158v), published in 1540. The heading translates as 'the foundation of the mine disclosed', and the powder chamber to the left is identified as 'the place of greatest effect'. (From *The Pirotechnia of Vannoccio Biringuccio*, translated and edited by Cyril Stanley Smith and Martha Teach Gnudi, MIT Press, 1943. Reproduced by courtesy of the MIT Press)

13. Drawing from Gabriello Busca's *Della Espugnatione* (1585, pages 136–7), illustrating a discourse on plotting the length, direction and depth of a mine aimed at the face of an angle bastion. (BL 62.b.15. Reproduced by permission of the British Library)

1524. In this text the need to bend or curve the gallery leading from the powder chamber is not mentioned.

A little more detail was provided with the publication in 1540 of the influential work *De la Pirotechnia* by Vannoccio Biringuccio. The fourth chapter of the tenth book of this volume deals with the military mine and includes a single woodcut (figure 12). Biringuccio writes approvingly of the awesome power of the underground mine, acknowledging Francesco di Giorgio as the inventor of the explosive form, and citing Navarro's works at the siege of Castel dell'Ovo in 1503 as the most destructive feat of mining ever. Biringuccio clearly considers his own exposition to be definitive, dismissing any further discussion of the topic as 'windy and useless verbiage'. However, his treatment of mining was rather brief and of limited value. For one thing, he does not indicate how miners digging the meandering gallery of his illustration had even the slightest chance of proceeding in the right direction for the correct distance in order to connect with the target. Also, his mining method was only too easily intercepted and eliminated by countermining. It was left to other experts in the sixteenth century to analyse the matter of mine construction in a more scientific way, with real practical value.

One of the most technical contributions was contained in the volume *Della Espugnatione et Difesa delle Fortezze* by Gabriello Busca, published in Turin in 1585. By this stage, the coiling gallery of Biringuccio's imagination had been superseded by linear or right-angled

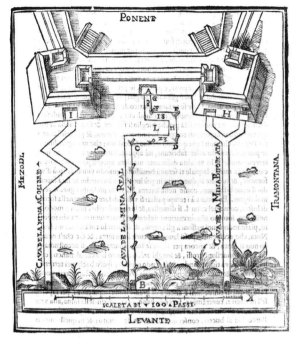

14. Mine variations illustrated by Luys Collado in *Practica Manuale* (1606 edition, page 211). From left to right: zigzagged, right-angled and branched (forked) galleries. (BL 534.i.7. Reproduced by permission of the British Library)

models, illustrated with charmingly scenic woodcuts (figure 13). Busca gives advice on how to avoid mistakes when digging a mine, and other instructions for getting the best results. In book two of the volume, he considers mining from the besieged garrison's point of view.

Another very detailed work, the definitive discourse on mining at the end of the sixteenth century, was contained in a volume by Luys Collado, first published in Spain in 1592, but which appeared in an Italian edition in 1606 as *Practica Manuale de Artilleria*. Much of treatise five was devoted to the subject of mining, three forms of which are depicted in one of Collado's illustrations (figure 14).

It was quickly accepted that the design of fortifications had to adapt to the dangers posed by powerful mobile cannon. The new military architecture, based on defences incorporating angle bastions, four-sided projecting works for mounting artillery, came to be known as the *trace italienne*. The first Italian treatise on the new method was written in 1554 by Giovanni Zanchi. The bastion provided an effective means of mounting cannon on ramparts and was designed to absorb the impact of heavy artillery fire, but its angular plan made it much more vulnerable to mining than the circular mural towers of medieval defences. The improvements could not ignore the need to provide extra defences against enemy miners. These took the form of countermine galleries incorporated into the masonry walls of the new fortifications. The earliest versions were multifunctional, and not specifically designed for detecting mining

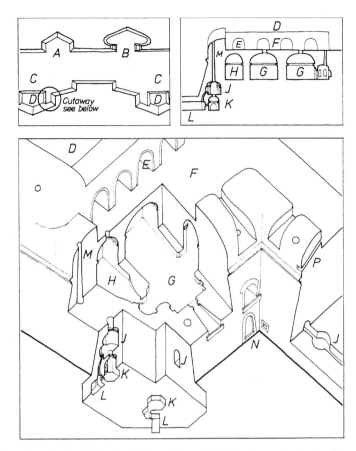

15. Drawings of a double bastion design at Porta Ardeatina, Rome, devised by Antonio da Sangallo the Younger in 1542. Plan view (top left), section (top right), and cutaway axonometric view (below). The elements of the prefabricated countermine system are: (J) countermine chamber; (K) *pozzi* or well shafts; (L) countermine gallery; and (M) ventilation flues. (From Simon Pepper and Nick Adams, *Firearms and Fortifications*, 1986. Reproduced by permission of the University of Chicago Press)

works. They were at the level of the ditch floor and, as such, were not deep enough. Significant progress was made by the work of the architect Antonio da Sangallo the Younger. His designs at Porta Ardeatina, Rome, in 1542 incorporated a countermine system that included lower chambers (*pozzi*), from which galleries could be extended as required (figure 15).

Impact and role in siege warfare

Many sieges of the sixteenth century combined heavy bombardment with intensive mining work. This strategy characterises numerous Turkish sieges of the period, the Turks displaying what Charles Oman

16. Illustration of the explosion of a mine under the Land Gate at Famagusta, Cyprus, during the siege of 1571. This was one of a great many sieges where Turkish mastery of mining technology was very ably demonstrated. (Topkapi Palace Museum)

described as an 'addiction' to great feats of mining (figure 16). The combined effects of battery and mining carried the day at Belgrade in 1521, and at the monumental siege of Rhodes in 1522. Before they were finally overcome, the defenders at Rhodes courageously resisted Turkish mining with a supreme countermining effort under the supervision of chief engineer Gabriele Tadini da Martinengo. Tadini invented a mine-detection device consisting of a stressed parchment diaphragm on to which small bells were mounted, which tinkled in response to any subterranean vibration. He also bored a series of 'spiral vents' that harmlessly dispersed some of the Turkish explosions. This run of Turkish victories was secured at the cost of considerable losses on their own side. The turning point came at Vienna in 1529. Again, after intensive bombardment and mining, assaults were launched, but this time the Turks were compelled to give up and retreat.

Instead of going down the route of the trebuchet – into military oblivion – the advent of gunpowder revitalised the art of siege mining, modernising a weapon that was as old as the first walled town. Gunpowder made the mine deadlier, more dreaded and more widespread than before, but it was far more dangerous to its own side, requiring much greater training and skill in the execution, and so was more likely to end in failure.

5
Tudor Britain and Ireland

Henry VIII of England gained first-hand experience of siege warfare during his expedition to France in 1513. The town of Thérouanne was besieged, and attacked by means of battery and mining. During the siege the garrison set off an explosive countermine (*camouflet*) that killed several of its own men. In 1544 the king led another expedition to France. Two hundred miners travelled with the expedition. Boulogne was besieged for five weeks. Approach trenches were dug by the sappers and, after an assault on the main wall failed, mines were dug in several places. The mining was supervised by an Italian engineer, Birolamo da Treviso, who was killed during the siege. A mine fired on 4th September 1544 damaged a bastion called Fleming's Tower, and another one on 11th September threw masonry out, killing some of the sappers. These operations were only a qualified success, but in any case the garrison was persuaded to surrender by 14th September. Apart from this campaign, we hear of English miners in the service of France at Saint-Quentin in 1557, and at Thionville the following year.

As well as the forays into France, English forces were occasionally drawn into Scottish politics, and the border region was always hotly contested. In terms of mining, the most significant siege was that of St Andrews Castle in Fife. This was very protracted, dragging on for over fourteen months until a conclusion was reached in July 1547. The castle was besieged by the Earl of Arran following its seizure by a group responsible for the murder of Cardinal David Beaton, a bitter opponent of Henry VIII. Although the castle was built on rock, mining and countermining were initiated near the fore tower on its southern side. What makes these galleries unique is that they were discovered intact in the nineteenth century during roadworks and may be viewed by visitors today. The underground chambers consist of a sloping mine aligned north–south, the northern limit of which is broken into by a countermine at a higher level, aligned south-west to north-east (figure 17). The mine was 1.8 metres wide and 2.1 metres high, making it remarkably spacious and impressive in scale. Being on the higher level, the counterminers would have had the option of flooding out their opponents once the breakthrough had been made, and something like this must have occurred, stopping the oncoming mine in its tracks. The digging of lateral galleries from the mine-head was in progress when the miners were forced to abandon the work. Elsewhere in the castle, to the west of the fore tower, there are two trial countermine shafts, which were sunk by the garrison to establish the location of the enemy mine (figure 17). These were

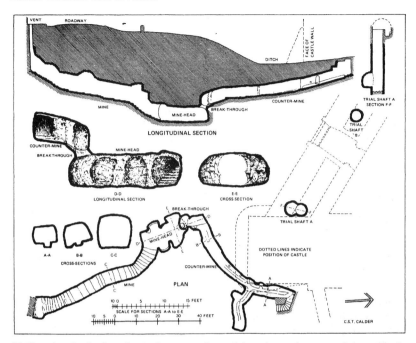

17. Plan, longitudinal section and cross-sections of the mine and countermine outside the fore tower at the southern end of St Andrews Castle, Fife. Also plotted are two trial shafts, A and B, located on the western side of the fore tower. (© Crown copyright: Royal Commission on the Ancient and Historical Monuments of Scotland)

abandoned in favour of the countermine on the eastern side of the fore tower, although the existence of a branch driven towards the east shows that the counterminers were still uncertain from which direction the enemy was advancing before they finally settled on a course to the south-west that eventually resulted in the break-through (figure 18).

The English re-conquest of Ireland, which was completed during the Nine Years' War (1594–1603), involved a considerable amount of action leading to the capture of numerous strongholds and castles. The use of covered mining under portable shelters known as 'sows' was fairly common. In 1595 at Sligo Castle the English under Sir Richard Bingham constructed 'engines for demolishing castles', which were sows built of reused materials, covered on the outside with oxhides, and mounted on wheels. The vehicles were drawn up to the edge of the walls and the sappers within started to bore away at the masonry. The garrison responded by raining stones upon the sows and discharging handguns until the English were beaten out of their 'wall-destroying domiciles' and abandoned the siege. The sow was an easy target for resourceful defenders and was prone to destruction. At Liscaghan in County Kerry in 1600, the warders sallied out and tore the sow to pieces. The following year at Castle-ny-Park, County Cork, the sow was crushed by stones.

Gallery mining would have been more effective in Ireland but was very rarely attempted there, probably because of a lack of men with experience in this type of endeavour. The concept of building a gallery beneath the ground, supported by timber props, was revealed in an unusual way at Lord Fitzmaurice's castle at Lixnaw, County Kerry, in 1600. Here the castle's owner had the building deliberately 'sapped and underset with props' so that the structure could be destroyed by springing the mine to prevent its occupation by an English garrison. However, Sir Charles Wilmot took the castle by surprise and the threatened destruction was averted. In pursuit of Fitzmaurice, Wilmot came to the castle of Listowel, County Kerry, and placed it under siege in November 1600. Gallery mining was commenced, and the garrison surrendered when Wilmot threatened to explode a mine driven underneath the cellar of the

building. The action at Listowel is significant as the first definite example of the use of gallery mining at a siege in Ireland, and the written account of the siege was supported by a remarkable discovery in 1986, when a tunnel was revealed in the course of digging for a drainage scheme. This feature is most likely the second of the two mines instigated by Wilmot in 1600, and further archaeological investigation at Listowel would certainly reveal

18. Interior view of the large rock-cut mine at St Andrews Castle, dating from the siege of 1546. (© Crown copyright. Reproduced courtesy of Historic Scotland)

19. Interior view of the tunnel at Listowel Castle, County Kerry, revealed during the course of drainage improvement work in November 1986. (Photograph: Michael Ward. Reproduced by courtesy of Listowel Town Council)

more evidence relating to this siege (figure 19).

There was a large crop of military literature produced in the Elizabethan period. Peter Whitehorne's book *Certain Waies for the Orderying of Souldiers in Battleray*, published in 1562, is of significance as the first work in English on the subject of mining. However, Whitehorne did not write from personal experience, and chapter 28, 'Of Muynes', was lifted word for word, without acknowledgement, from Biringuccio's *De la Pirotechnia* of 1540. However, as a translation rather than an original study, Whitehorne's volume is still of importance. On a related subject, Paul Ive's *The Practise of Fortification*, published in 1589, reveals an awareness of the menace that the offensive mine represented. Ive was also concerned with the nature of countermines, which if poorly established could weaken the foundations of a wall.

The general public of the day clearly had a good grasp of what miners working at a siege were trying to achieve. Because of this broad awareness, Shakespeare's *Henry V*, first performed in 1600, could contain a comical scene based on mining and countermining at the siege of Harfleur that had meaning even for an audience not composed of veterans back from the wars (act III, scene 2, 52–60). In the same way, the metaphorical allusion to the explosive countermine ('But I will delve one yard below their mines/And blow them at the moon!'), to be found in a speech in *Hamlet*, dating from 1603 (act IV, scene 3, 208–9), must have been penned in the belief that the ordinary person would understand and be impressed by such an image.

6
The early seventeenth century

Warfare in the Netherlands lasted almost continuously from 1566 to 1648, during which time a new, scientific method of siege warfare was developed. The method had five stages, beginning with a double ring enclosing the besieged town, known as lines of contravallation (facing the besieged fortress) and circumvallation (facing the open country and ready to repel an army of relief). These trenches were opened by ordinary workmen (pioneers) out of range of the garrison's fire, working parallel to the town wall or ditch, the trenches protected by parapets thrown up by shovelling soil into wicker baskets (gabions). In the second stage, approach trenches were dug and the initial siege batteries were established. Third, the pioneers dug their way to the lip of the ditch in another series of approach trenches (saps), made in zigzagging lines to prevent enfilading fire from decimating the workforce. When the saps were close to the outer edge of the ditch, another line parallel with the ditch was dug, with a parapet on the fortress side. The ramparts could be battered from this position, knocking out the garrison's cannon. The fourth stage involved crossing the ditch itself. This was done by filling it in to form a causeway and constructing a square-sectioned timber gallery, with an outer layer of earth and stones. If the masonry on the other side was already breached by cannon fire, an assault could begin once the gallery reached the far side of the ditch. If not, the fifth stage proceeded, which was the making of a breach by the expedient of 'attaching' a miner to the foundations for the purpose of excavating an explosive mine that could be fired underneath the masonry. Once the mine had created a breach, an assault could be attempted.

The scientific siege method went on to become further refined and perfected in the course of the seventeenth century, and the system, or something based very closely on it, served as the fundamental vehicle in siege warfare from this point onwards. The concept provided for what was in essence a completely updated form of covered mining, as the fifth stage before the assault itself was launched. The technique of filling in the ditch and spanning it with an overground gallery of timber precluded the digging of long subterranean tunnels. Although the end result was the planting of an explosive charge, the miner only went below ground at the face of the masonry, where he commenced digging into the foundations.

The role of mining remained traditional in the sense that it was introduced to support the work of artillery bombardment in breaching a wall, permitting an assault to be made, but generally only when initial battery and assaults failed. This meant that several sieges were spared the particular terrors of the mine – but there are many examples of mining at its most destructive. The siege of Haarlem by the Duke of Alva in 1573 was a particularly gruelling exercise lasting seven months. Mining was initiated by the Duke when casualties from assaults were too high, and coal miners from Liège were brought in for the work, although ultimately they achieved nothing. Hand-to-hand combat in mine and countermine took place over nine days at the siege of Sluis in 1587, and similar heroics were a feature of the bloody siege of Maastricht in 1579.

English military literature

In stark contrast with the situation on the Continent, which was a cauldron of conflict, and where many notable sieges were played out, the opening decades of the Stuart monarchy in the seventeenth century, until the eruption of civil war in the 1640s, were relatively quiet in Britain and Ireland. The military literature of the time was absorbed by the warfare in the Netherlands. A work by Richard Norwood entitled *Fortification, or Architecture Military*, published in 1640, provided detailed instructions on the making of Dutch-style earthen fortifications, down to the organisation of the workforce and the time involved in construction. The most exhaustive treatment of the Dutch military system was Henry Hexham's *The Principles of the Art Militare, as Practised in the Warres of the United Netherlands*, published in 1637, with parts two and three added in 1639 and 1640. All three parts were reprinted in 1642–3 to provide much-needed military instruction at the onset of the Civil War in England.

In many ways the most comprehensive single volume available to officers at the beginning of the wars of the 1640s was Robert Ward's *Anima'adversions of Warre*, published in 1639. Again, the contest in the Low Countries provided the inspiration for the work, and a lengthy account of the great siege of Breda in 1624 was included. As with Norwood's contemporary volume, there is much on the topic of fortification theory and design, but Ward goes further, with analysis on the attack and defence of places, including the use of mines and countermines. In a separate section, Ward gives instructions and rules concerning the mining of a bulwark (figure 20).

Ward's commentary on mining fairly closely mirrors the guidelines set down by experts such as Collado at the end of the previous century. What is significant here is that although 'attaching' a miner to the foot of a wall came from the fifth stage of the scientific or formal siege, Ward's advice on the digging of long gallery mines is aimed at a situation in which the methodical imposition of the steps of the scientific system was not possible. Only great armies, often with a monarch personally in

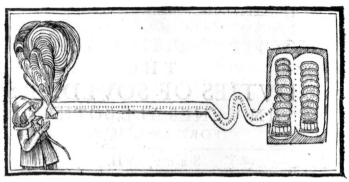

20. Woodcut diagram of an explosive mine from Robert Ward's *Anima'adversions of Warre* (1639, page 149). (BL 718.i.19. Reproduced by permission of the British Library)

command, had resources enough to enclose a walled town with lines of contravallation and circumvallation, setting the process of systematic reduction in motion. In practice, much fighting in the Netherlands, and, as it turned out, in the English Civil War and the Irish Confederate War, was conducted by lesser opposed forces. The context in which gallery mines of this type might be called for was likely to be one in which a military division, without heavy ordnance, wished to breach and assault a detached field fortification, a strong house or an old castle. Therefore, Ward's discussion of gallery mining was highly relevant to the realities of warfare in the mid seventeenth century, in which scattered places of strength and strategic value had to be reduced by forces with limited means.

The English Civil War

It has been calculated by Charles Carlton that of 645 military actions in England during the Civil War period 198 were sieges. Almost every kind of tactic was used in the course of the war, in sieges that ranged from rapid assaults on isolated churches and manor houses to lengthy investments of large and heavily fortified cities. In the course of the Civil War, artillery came to play an increasingly prominent role during sieges, and the deployment of larger and more numerous cannon became the key to successful siege operations. The New Model Army was supplied with a large siege train, and these guns had great significance for the outcome of the war. The commanders of the New Model Army favoured the siege methods of bombardment and assault, which, while often bloody, were valued above the slow and steady waste associated with the longer siege.

Some form of mining was an aspect of a number of sieges of the Civil

War, and the use of civilian miners from coalfields or ironworks is well documented. In the early stages of the war it was not unknown for the antiquated movable engine or 'sow' to be brought into play, as at Corfe Castle, Dorset, in 1643. However, these archaic devices were quickly superseded by more effective underground mining, and, in general, burnt-prop springing was replaced by explosive charges, the first British example of which occurred at the siege of Lichfield Close, Staffordshire, in 1643. Mining and countermining were important elements of King Charles's unsuccessful siege of Gloucester in 1643. The excavation in 1988 of a Royalist approach trench or sap at Southgate Street highlights the potential for the discovery of further archaeological evidence relating to the siege of the city. Evidence for the effects of explosive mining during the siege of York in 1644 can be seen at St Mary's Tower, which was blown up by a mine and subsequently rebuilt with thinner masonry (figure 21). At Newcastle upon Tyne, a funnel-shaped crater discovered during archaeological excavations has been interpreted as the location of a Civil War mine from the siege of 1644. Well-documented mining operations occurred at the sieges of a number of castles, including Wardour Castle, Wiltshire, in 1643 and Sherborne Castle, Dorset, in 1645. At Pontefract Castle, West Yorkshire, there are three countermine

21. St Mary's Tower, York, was blown up by a mine during the siege of 1644 and was subsequently reconstructed with slightly thinner masonry. The thickness of the original wall can be seen along the left-hand edge of the tower. (Photograph: Kenneth Wiggins)

22. The start of a horizontal tunnel at the bottom of the countermine shaft below the Elizabeth Chapel at Pontefract Castle, West Yorkshire, dating from the siege of 1645. (Reproduced by courtesy of the West Yorkshire Archaeological Service)

shafts cut into the sandstone bedrock from the siege of 1645 (figure 22). One of the shafts contained a pickaxe, and another an iron bar or stake used for digging.

Mining was also very widely employed by the Parliamentarian forces to consolidate victory and to prevent captured strongholds from being used as centres of renewed Royalist activity. The policy involved the deliberate destruction or 'slighting' of a large number of strategic fortifications by undermining and blowing up parts of the masonry. The policy was implemented with characteristic precision and thoroughness across the country, from Helmsley Castle in North Yorkshire to Nunney Castle in Somerset. The remains of several castles bear the signs of slighting caused by undermining, for example the dramatically ruptured south-west gatehouse at Corfe Castle, Dorset (figure 23).

Ireland 1642–8

The relative tranquillity that Ireland enjoyed after the end of the Nine Years' War in 1603 was shattered forty years later with the outbreak of trouble in Ulster in October 1641. The flame of rebellion spread rapidly to ignite the rest of the country. As in Britain, sieges were a very prominent dimension of the conflict. Attempts at undermining walls were fairly frequent but, as was traditional in Ireland, this usually took

23. View of the shattered south-west gatehouse of Corfe Castle, Dorset, one of the most dramatic examples of the 'slighting' of Royalist strongholds instigated by the Parliamentarian authorities in 1646, whereby miners rendered the main defences useless. (National Trust Photograph Library/Matthew Antrobus)

the form of covered mining involving the construction of portable 'sows', and several operations of this type are well documented, such as the first siege of Ballyallia Castle, County Clare, in 1642. However, the digging of deep galleries could be attempted if skilled workmen with civilian experience of mining were available, and these conditions prevailed in Limerick when the Catholic army in Munster was admitted to the city at the beginning of May 1642. The English citizens took shelter behind the walls of the King's castle, which was immediately besieged by the Irish forces. The events of the siege were chronicled in great detail by contemporaries, but an entirely new insight on the episode was possible as a result of excavations at the castle in the 1990s, which produced the most significant archaeological evidence relating to siege mining discovered so far, highlighting the great potential that archaeological investigation has to broaden our knowledge of how mines were constructed and used in the course of a siege.

The Catholic army drawn around the castle did not possess any large cannon that could be used to batter the castle and make a breach in its wall. The workers from the royal silver mines in Munster who came to Limerick for safety at the beginning of 1642 were now divided equally between the besieging Irish forces and the besieged English garrison, which allowed mining and countermining to form the backbone of the operations of the siege. Mining activity commenced along the eastern

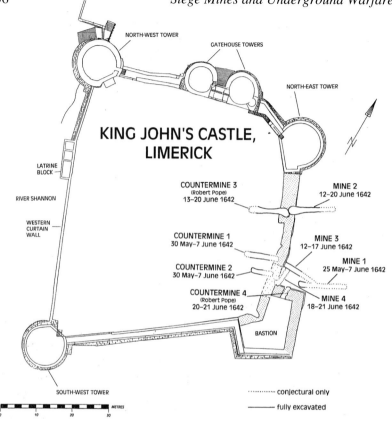

KING JOHN'S CASTLE, LIMERICK

NORTH-WEST TOWER

GATEHOUSE TOWERS

NORTH-EAST TOWER

LATRINE BLOCK

RIVER SHANNON

WESTERN CURTAIN WALL

COUNTERMINE 3 (Robert Pope) 13–20 June 1642

MINE 2 12–20 June 1642

COUNTERMINE 1 30 May–7 June 1642

MINE 3 12–17 June 1642

MINE 1 25 May–7 June 1642

COUNTERMINE 2 30 May–7 June 1642

COUNTERMINE 4 (Robert Pope) 20–21 June 1642

MINE 4 18–21 June 1642

BASTION

SOUTH-WEST TOWER

METRES
0   10   20   30

.... conjectural only
———— fully excavated

24. Plan of the mines and countermines excavated in 1990–1 at King John's Castle, Limerick, dating from the siege of 1642. (© Kenneth Wiggins)

side of the castle on 25th May and towards the southern side on 1st June and was met by determined countermining on both fronts, until breaches were successfully made on the eastern side that brought about the surrender of the castle to the Irish army on 23rd June. Altogether, eleven Irish mines were constructed in the course of the siege, and eight countermines were instigated by the garrison. Contemporary accounts credit a miner named Robert Pope with the construction of the final two countermines. Large-scale archaeological excavations on the eastern side of the castle in 1990–1 revealed the remains of several of these structures, and a total of more than three hundred well-preserved timbers was recovered (figure 24). These included many of the baseplates and props of the frames that were used to support the galleries as they advanced into the depths, both outside and inside the castle's perimeter.

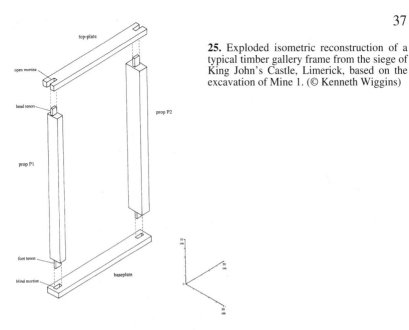

top-plate

open mortise

head tenon

prop P1

foot tenon

baseplate

blind mortise

prop P2

25. Exploded isometric reconstruction of a typical timber gallery frame from the siege of King John's Castle, Limerick, based on the excavation of Mine 1. (© Kenneth Wiggins)

Towards the climax of the siege, Mine 3 reached the base of the eastern curtain wall by around 17th June. Many of the timbers in this structure were charred as the result of a fire that was set within the gallery on the afternoon of 21st June. This mine contained a substantial raised floor that was composed of a great many timber planks, two of which were over 3 metres in length. A discarded iron crowbar used in the digging of the mine was found beneath the surface of the raised floor.

The quality of the excavated evidence at Limerick is such that we can form an accurate picture of how the mines and countermines were constructed. When a gallery was to be opened at the bottom of an entrance shaft, the first rectangular timber frame was established. A frame was made up of four members: a baseplate, mortised at both ends, which was laid transversely across the floor of the mine; two vertical props for the sides, each with a foot tenon that was inserted into a baseplate mortise; a horizontal top-plate completed the frame by connecting the opposed pair of props and was secured by mortise-and-tenon joinery (figures 25 and 26). The frames were installed along the length of a gallery at intervals of between 32 cm and 76 cm. The sectional dimensions of the galleries, controlled by the size of the timber frames, varied between 1.16 metres and 1.61 metres in width and by between 1.4 metres and 1.6 metres in height. To prevent subsidence, the overhead gaps between the frames were filled with slotted-in timber planks, supported by the top-plates, and the side gaps were often covered

26. Detail of the well-preserved tenon at the foot of prop P11 (oak) from Countermine 1 at King John's Castle, Limerick. The tenon is 7.5 cm long, 8 cm wide and 4.5 cm thick. (Photograph: Kenneth Wiggins)

with pointed timber strips, inserted between adjacent pairs of props (figures 27 and 28).

The tactics used throughout the siege of Limerick Castle show that the besiegers had no time for the formal procedures of the scientific siege that were typical of large-scale operations on the Continent. Indeed, the mines themselves were of the outmoded 'burnt-prop' variety that belonged to the medieval era and made no concessions to contemporary explosive mining technology. Gallery mining employing the skills of miners from the silver mines in Munster occurred again at the sieges of Ballinakill, County Laois, and Birr Castle, County Offaly, both in 1643. These operations were also

27. Plan of the excavated gallery of Countermine 1 at King John's Castle, Limerick, with northern and southern elevations. (© Kenneth Wiggins)

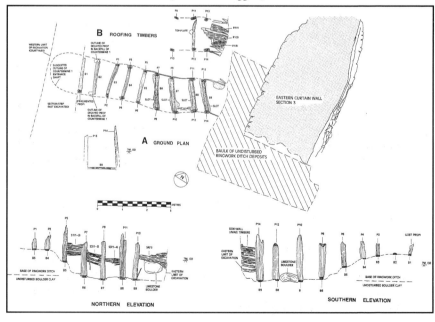

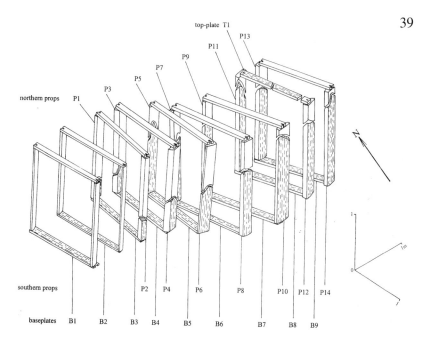

top-plate T1

P13

P11

P9

P7

P5

P3

northern props P1

southern props P2 P4 P6 P8 P10 P12 P14

baseplates B1 B2 B3 B4 B5 B6 B7 B8 B9

28. Isometric reconstruction of the nine excavated timber frames of the Countermine 1 gallery at King John's Castle, Limerick. (© Kenneth Wiggins)

carried out with little reference to the theories of formal siege warfare that were currently practised on the Continent. However, in early 1645 Duncannon Fort, County Wexford, was besieged by the Irish with the assistance of a French engineer, Nicholas Lalloe, and his system of trenches and batteries was recognisably continental in its planning and execution. The attack culminated in mining before the place was surrendered. Although the fort was subsequently rebuilt, indicators visible from the air in the environs of Duncannon suggest that sub-surface evidence for the siege survives, and this appears to be a site that could one day make an important contribution to the subject of siege warfare in Ireland if archaeological excavations of the 1645 siege lines were to take place.

The reduction of Ireland that came about with the campaigning of Oliver Cromwell in 1649–50 was accompanied by much intensive siege warfare, but there was little or no recourse to undermining tactics. There is some evidence for the deliberate destruction or 'slighting' of selected Irish confederate fortifications, mirroring the Parliamentarian policy in England, as for example the undermining and blowing up of the keep at Clonmacnoise Castle, County Offaly, and the partial demolition of Clough Oughter Castle, County Cavan.

7
The later seventeenth century and the eighteenth century

In northern Europe in the latter part of the seventeenth century the theory and practice of fortification and fortress warfare were synonymous with the name of the exceptional French engineer Sébastien Le Prestre de Vauban (1633–1707). At the siege of Maastricht in 1673 Vauban perfected the system of trench attack by linking the zigzag approaches with enclosing lines called parallels. Because mining was a key instrument in breaching the strongest and most heavily defended walls, he went on in 1679 to create the first permanent company of French miners. Vauban was a prolific writer and his manuscripts were carefully studied and immensely influential. These included his definitive works *Traité des Sièges et de l'Attaque des Places* (1704) and *Traité de la Défense des Places* (1706), both of which were finally published in Paris in 1829. The fortifications of Vauban's time were the most formidable yet devised, and his numerous works contributed greatly to France's defences, many of which remain impressive (figure 29). Vauban's expertise in constructing fortifications was matched by his grasp of siegecraft. His ideas on this subject were meticulously

29. View of a damaged ravelin (since restored), constructed by Vauban in the late seventeenth century, at Le Quesnoy, France, exposing part of a countermine gallery within. (Photograph: Christopher Duffy)

considered, and the place of the miner in the reduction of complex defences was an important feature of the complete picture.

During the progress of a siege, when the outworks were occupied by the besieging troops and batteries established on the edge of the ditch, it was time to place miners on the inner wall. Vauban recognised two ways of achieving this: first, by an older method that involved laying against the wall heavy beams, which were then screened to provide cover; second, by a newer method, which was to use cannon, placed opposite the position to be mined, to make a crack in the wall. The first method was hazardous as the beams were exposed to objects cast down from the ramparts, which could destroy the mining effort. Vauban advocated the second alternative, as the guns opened the mouth of the mine, allowing the miner immediately to begin working well inside the wall, up to 1.5–1.8 metres inside according to Vauban, protecting him from fire bombs dropped from above. The cannon could also be used to destroy any countermines within the thickness of the wall, and once the mine was exploded they could be used to fire into the breach. Vauban stated that the quantity of powder used in a mine should be proportionate to the mass that was to be blown up, to the depth of the mine, and to the size of the gap that was to be opened. He laid down rules for engaging with the enemy should the work be interrupted by countermining. He recommended the destruction of countermine galleries with small explosive charges (*camouflets*). Permanent countermine galleries made within the walls of fortifications could have several branches in different directions. These were generally 1.2–1.35 metres wide and 1.5–1.65 metres high, of masonry walls and arches.

There were different types of mine, depending on what was required. Vauban classified these as simple mines, double mines and triple or trefoil mines (figure 30: 1, 2, 3). The simple mine had only a single gallery and a single chamber (where the explosives were placed). The double or T-mine divided into two equal branches. The triple or trefoil mine had the two chambers of the double mine, with the addition of a third chamber run from the centre. Round or square chambers were best, with a level base, and raised, vaulted ceilings. Vauban recommended that the chambers should be dropped by between 30 cm and 45 cm below the gallery. If water was encountered, the chamber could be placed at a level higher than the gallery. Galleries were better driven with right-angled elbows rather than pushed straight ahead. They were between 0.9 metres and 1.05 metres in width, and 1.5 metres in height, the earth supported by wooden frames.

Vauban noted that it was formerly the practice to charge mines by placing powder barrels in the chambers from which the covers had been removed. An alternative practice was to use bags of powder, which

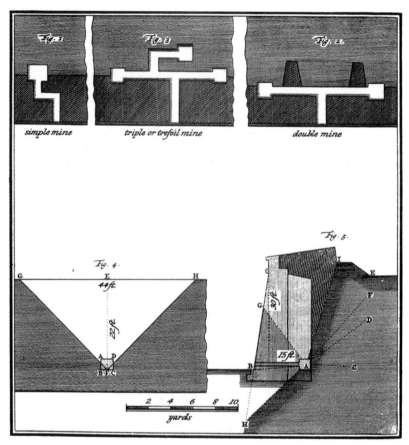

30. Diagram of mines by Sébastien Le Prestre de Vauban, originally from writings of 1667–72, published posthumously in 1740. The illustration shows three types of mine (Figures 1–3), the inverted cone caused by the explosion of a mine (Figure 4), and the undermining of a wall 9.1 metres high by a gallery 4.6 metres long (Figure 5). (From Sébastien Le Prestre de Vauban, *A Manual of Siegecraft and Fortification*, edited and translated by G. A. Rothrock, 1968. Reproduced by permission of the University of Michigan Press)

were piled up and then slashed with a knife. Vauban preferred a method that involved inserting a wooden floor in the chamber, which was covered with a layer of straw and coarse cloth, over which the powder was distributed in piles. This way the powder ignited more quickly and distributed the blast more evenly. The charge could also be placed in a strong wooden box, lined with straw and empty sandbags, to keep out damp. The fuse was a cloth tube about 4 cm in diameter, known as a *saucisson*, loosely filled with powder. A hole was made in the side of the powder box to let the *saucisson* pass through, the end of which was fixed to the bottom by a wooden peg. The box was covered with planks and props, wedged as tightly as possible. To keep damp away from the *saucisson*, it was laid on a small trough, called an *auget*, made of 9 cm boards, with straw added and a wooden cover nailed on top, extending all the way from the chamber to the gallery entrance.

Prior to the charge being set off, the mine was carefully tamped or sealed. This was done with timber beams bonded together, tightly fixed with wooden wedges; stones, earth and dung were also brought in and rammed hard to stop up the gallery. Several rows of these beams were set along its length. Any spaces or gaps in the tamping could seriously weaken the effects of the subsequent springing of the mine. Once blocked in this way, the mine was ready to be primed and blown. The hole made by the eruption of earth following the explosion of a mine was known as the 'excavation' and had the shape of an inverted cone (figure 30: 4). Vauban, in articulating his calculations for maximising the effects of mining, argued, for example, that for a rampart 9 metres high to be

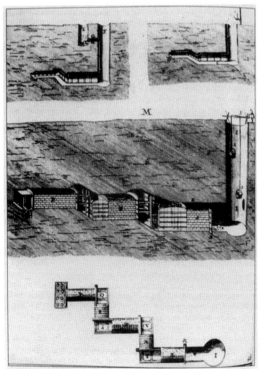

31. Diagrams of mine shafts and galleries from *Mémoires d'Artillerie* (page 48) by Pierre Surirey de Saint-Rémy, published in 1702. Three mines are illustrated in section: one with a second shaft and fire for ventilation (top left), another with ventilation by windsail (top right), and a sophisticated mine incorporating several right-angle turns (centre), with a plan view at the bottom. An English version of Saint-Rémy's writings was published by Henry Manningham in 1752 under the title *A Complete Treatise of Mines*. (From Christopher Duffy, *Fire and Stone*, 1996. Reproduced by permission of Greenhill Books)

blown up successfully a gallery 4.5 metres in length had to be made (figure 30: 5).

Apart from the problems of how to establish mines under a wall and how to achieve the optimum effect, the digging of long galleries could lead to difficulties of ventilation, which could be addressed by the sinking of an auxiliary shaft, connected to the main shaft, in which a fire was lit to draw stale air from the gallery, a method used centuries earlier in the Iron Age salt mines at Hallstatt in Austria (figure 31). Air could be forced into a gallery via a hose, connected at the surface to a large bellows. The tools commonly used in mining included augers of various kinds, levers or crowbars of different types, needles and chisels for working in rock, spades, shovels, wheelbarrows, sledge-hammers, masons' hammers, pickaxes, mattocks, plumb lines and levels.

Many of the greatest sieges in history belong to a long period of intense warfare in Europe, spanning the final decades of the seventeenth century and continuing into the middle decades of the eighteenth century. Many of these featured the deployment of mines and countermines, which were now more scientifically conceived than ever before. The Turks dug and mined furiously at the Burg and Löbel bastions during the siege of Vienna in 1683, until the arrival of an army of relief resulted in the lifting of the siege. Underground combat was a feature of the siege of Turin in 1706. Later in the eighteenth century a supercharged mine known as the 'globe of compression' was developed, named after the globe formed by particles of earth when acted upon by an explosion, which marshalled the destructive potential of mining even further. The devastation associated with this type of mining was unleashed at Frederick the Great's siege of Schweidnitz in Poland in 1762, and at the siege of Valenciennes in France in 1793.

8
The nineteenth and twentieth centuries

Military engineering became increasingly professional during the nineteenth century. In the British army several artificer companies had been established by 1812 for work on fortifications, but the companies were much less effective in field operations and changes were needed. The Royal Engineer Establishment was started at Chatham, Kent, in 1812 to improve standards in military field engineering. Training here included large-scale practising of mining and countermining techniques and was realistic to the point of exploding a 500 kg mine during siege operations in 1877 in the otherwise quiet district of Brompton (figure 32).

The improved qualities of the British military engineers were exported around the world with the expansion and consolidation of the empire. Opportunities to put mining skills to the test arose in India at the siege of Bhurtpore, which commenced late in 1825. The Bengal Sappers and Miners, who formed part of the British besieging force, dug and exploded a series of mines without creating breaches that could be assaulted. Finally, the long-necked or Pathian bastion was undermined and set with a 4535 kg charge. When this was sprung on 18th January 1826, the massive bastion was ripped out of the ground and flung into the air, and the city was taken by storming attack.

32. A remarkable photograph of the detonation of a 500 kg mine in a normally peaceful Kent suburb in 1877, unleashed in the interests of authenticity at the climax of siege operations practised by the specialists of the Royal Engineers, Brompton Barracks, Chatham. (Reproduced by kind permission of the Institution of Royal Engineers)

The position in India was reversed during the great mutiny of 1857, when the first instances of native mining occurred at the siege of Lucknow. The British countermined, using Cornishmen supervised by Captain Fulton, the garrison engineer. This officer made a name for himself by listening for the approach of the enemy mines, revolver in hand, waiting for them to break through (figure 33). Fulton stopped every mine of the enemy but was killed in action on 14th September. Twenty mines were driven towards the defences, of which only three were exploded. Countermining was on an enormous scale, with 1 km of gallery constructed by the end of the siege. The shafts were an average of 2.4 metres in depth, and the galleries, usually without timber shoring, 90 cm high (with an arched roof) and 60 cm wide.

At the onset of the American Civil War, a corps of engineers was established in the Confederate army, including a company of sappers, miners and pontoniers (bridge-builders). Each engineer officer was to carry, along with the army's own rules and regulations, a copy of Vauban's *Fortifications*. Colonel Paul Stevens wrote a work entitled *Notes on Sapping and Mining*, which was due to have been published in 1864 but was withheld through lack of funding. The most famous instance of mining in American military history occurred in the course of the siege of Petersburg, Virginia, in 1864. In considering ways of breaking the deadlock, General Ambrose Burnside conceived the idea

33. 'Lying in Wait': a romantic contemporary portrayal of Captain George Fulton, Bengal Engineers, seated in a countermine during the siege of Lucknow, India, in 1857. (© First published in 1933 by the Institution of Royal Engineers in the book *The Military Engineer in India* by Lieutenant-Colonel Edward Sandes)

34. Contemporary illustration of miners of the 48th Pennsylvania Veteran Volunteer Infantry digging the great mine during the siege of Petersburg, 1864. (© Corbis)

of using coal miners from Pennsylvania to dig a tunnel, 152 metres in length, below Confederate lines (figure 34). The chamber at the end of this gallery was packed with 3.6 tonnes of explosives and the charge was ignited on 30th June, creating a colossal crater. The ensuing 'battle of the crater' did not prove to be decisive, as the Union soldiers were unsure of how to follow up the explosion and failed to capitalise on the stunned amazement of their opponents.

By this stage in history, the classic age of European siege warfare was over but, despite the changing times, the ancient craft of mining never became wholly obsolete. At the siege of Peking in 1900 the Chinese exploded two mines under the French Legation, severely damaging the defences. The garrison started a countermine, and further mines were successfully exploded before the siege was lifted with the arrival of relief. Indeed, the hour of the most extraordinary feats of mining and countermining still lay ahead.

The First World War
As the pace of battle in the Great War slowed down and lines of

entrenchments were defined, making front-line progress more difficult to achieve, it was only a matter of time before the possibilities offered by mining were explored by one side or the other. On 20th December 1914, near Festubert, the Germans made the first underground attack of the war, exploding ten mines. The follow-up assault was a complete success. The response on the British side was disorganised at first, but the contribution of John Norton Griffiths, an engineering contractor, was crucial. He was constructing a drainage scheme in Manchester, using a method for driving tunnels known as 'clay kicking' or 'working on the cross'. By this method, the digger did not use a pickaxe but sat on a narrow seat secured to a long wooden plank that was lodged at an angle at the end of the gallery; a short timber attachment supported the back, giving the plank a cross-like appearance. The 'clay kicker' kept both feet on a spade, which he used to cut out the subsoil face in front of him (figure 35). The spoil was gathered by his mate and passed along the gallery. This method of mining was swift and silent, with progress in good conditions of 3.65 metres or more per day, and would be ideal for use in Flanders, where the clay was deep and soft. Norton Griffiths was commissioned to enlist as many 'clay kickers' as he could find to comprise a new mining corps within the Royal Engineers, at a rate of six shillings a day. These were men with civilian mining experience in the London underground scheme and sewerage works, as well as coal and mineral miners. The 171st Tunnelling Company commenced mining at the Hill 60 area due east of Ypres in March 1915. Up to then the advantage in underground warfare had lain completely with the Germans, but on 17th April 1915 the British successfully sprung their first mines of the war, wired for electrical detonation, leaving characteristic craters in the ground and allowing an attack on the hill to be made. Mining and

35. Diagram of a 'clay kicker' of the Tunnelling Companies of the Western Front at work 'on the cross'. He uses a grafting tool at the mine face, a modified type of spade with projections for both feet. The miner sits on a long cross-like timber support placed within the gallery at an angle of 45 degrees. (From Captain W. Grant Grieve and B. Newman, *Tunnellers: The Story of the Tunnelling Companies, Royal Engineers, during the World War*, 1936 and 2001. Reproduced by courtesy of The Naval & Military Press)

36. German counterminers, digging an impressively large and well-framed gallery in 1916, pause momentarily. For the military miner, this was near the end of the line. (From Alexander Barrie, *War Underground*, published by Spellmount Limited and reproduced with grateful thanks)

countermining at Hill 60 were to continue for another two years.

Improvements in mining continued to be made as the war progressed. Better air pumps were produced and a listening device known as a geophone was developed. Later still, electric lighting was rigged up for the galleries. The demands for gunpowder and guncotton were such that alternative explosives were required, and the more powerful ammonal came to be used for charging the mines. This was a blasting explosive compound of nitroglycerine, ammonium nitrate and powdered aluminium. The men worked in conditions of extreme danger and discomfort. There was constant risk of explosions by enemy *camouflets*, small charges that were designed to wreck the opposition's mines without causing any damage on the surface, which released deadly carbon monoxide gas. Many miners were poisoned by gas from underground explosions, or buried under debris (figure 36).

The culmination of mining work during the war was the ambitious plan for the taking of Messines Ridge in 1917. Twenty-one mines were made ready for firing on 7th June, charged with over 450 tonnes of ammonal. On the day, nineteen were fired, generating a massive artificial earthquake, and allowed the ridge to be successfully captured by assault.

37. Mines in a landscape: aerial view from 1986 of pools marking the location of three of the nineteen Messines mines to the south of Ypres in Belgium that were detonated on 7th June 1917. From north to south: Maedelstede farm crater (A); the Peckham crater (B); and the giant Spanbroekmolen crater, or 'Pool of Peace' (C). (Reproduced by courtesy of Luchtfotografie Henderyckx–Izegem)

38. Close-up aerial photograph of the Spanbroekmolen crater. The cataclysmic force of its formation has bequeathed a legacy of tranquillity. The pool's surface reflects the long history of the military mine, now remote and stilled but never to be forgotten. (Reproduced by courtesy of Luchtfotografie Henderyckx–Izegem)

One of the two mines that was not detonated exploded during a thunderstorm in 1955. The location of the other remains unknown to this day.

The landscape of this area in south-west Belgium remains uniquely scarred by the unparalleled magnitude of the underground operations of 1915–17 (figures 37 and 38). The craters formed by the explosions are testaments not only to the endeavours of a particular campaign but also to the long history of tunnelling and mining in human conflict. The largest crater, Spanbroekmolen, or Lone Tree crater, measuring 131 metres across, resulted from the explosion of 41,275 kg of ammonal, set at the end of a gallery 521.3 metres in length: the greatest mine in history. The crater contains a lake that is 12.2 metres deep. The site, located about 8 km south of Ypres in south-west Belgium, was subsequently purchased by Lord Wakefield as a memorial. It is today known as the 'Pool of Peace' and has a commemorative headstone. The taking of Messines Ridge was a key moment in the First World War. Fighting conditions changed thereafter, and mining was discontinued on both sides, and has not been used by Western armies since.

9
Epilogue

Siege-related mining has today passed from the pages of military manuals into the realms of metaphor. We are frequently informed by television and newspapers of the politicians, officials and suchlike who in the course of some heated dispute or other complain about their authority or position being 'undermined'. It is doutbful whether any of the individuals invoking this cliché spare much thought for the origins of the term, or realise that they have casually alluded to what was one of the mainstays of siege warfare for thousands of years. Perhaps the image of a crouching man with dirt- and sweat-covered shoulders, teasing out a stone with his pickaxe in some dim subterranean cavity, flashes

39. Photograph of the inspection by Brigadier-General Richard T. Knowles (left) of the entrance to a Viet Cong tunnel complex discovered in the Cu Chi district in 1967. (From T. Mangold and J. Penycate, *The Tunnels of Cu Chi*, Pan Books, 1986. Reproduced by permission of the US Army)

40. Photograph from a newspaper feature entitled 'Tunnel rats badger away to beat bypass', published 28th December 1995, showing an anti-roads protester at work below Snelsmore Common, Newbury, Berkshire, in a tunnel 'decked out with pine walls'. (Copyright Express Newspapers)

across the mind's eye for an instant and then is lost. The undermining of walls by besieging armies may have been consigned into history, but something of its spirit remains embedded in our consciousness.

The tunnel has never been quite prepared to admit that its time is up. In the Far East, tunnels were made as hiding places by the Viet Minh in their war with the French. An extensive system was established by 1948, linking hamlets in occupied territory. This became the basis of the famous Cu Chi tunnel system, already with a total length of 200 km by the time of the arrival of the Americans in Vietnam in 1965 (figure 39). In 1995, a newspaper reporting on anti-road activities in Newbury, Berkshire, noted that the protesters, borrowing a 'secret tactic from the Viet Cong', had dug tunnels below the site of a proposed bypass (figure 40). The protesters may have been proud to follow the example of the Vietnamese fighters of the 1960s, but at the same time they were also saluting, however unwittingly, veterans of underground campaigns stretching back much further in time.

10
Further reading

Barratt, J. 'Battle of the Crater', *Military Illustrated*, 162 (November 2001), 48–55.

Barrie, A. *War Underground: The Tunnellers of the Great War.* Spellmount, Staplehurst, 2000 (originally published 1962).

Bradbury, J. *The Medieval Siege.* Boydell Press, Woodbridge, 1992.

Braun, H. *Bungay Castle: Historical Notes and Accounts of the Excavations.* Bungay Castle Trust, 1991 (originally published 1934–5).

Bury, J. 'The Early History of the Explosive Mine', *Fort*, 10 (1982), 23–30.

Bury, J. 'Early Writings on Fortifications and Siegecraft: 1502–1554', *Fort*, 13 (1985), 5–48.

Carlton, C. *Going to the Wars: The Experience of the British Civil Wars, 1638–1651.* Routledge, London, 1994.

Cima, K. *Reflections from the Bridge: The Victorian Sapper in Photographs.* Quotes Ltd, Whittlebury, 1994.

Corfis, I.A., and Wolfe, M. (editors). *The Medieval City under Siege.* Boydell Press, Woodbridge, 1995.

Duffy, C. *Siege Warfare: The Fortress in the Early Modern World, 1494–1660.* Routledge & Kegan Paul, London, 1979.

Duffy, C. *The Fortress in the Age of Frederick the Great, 1660–1789: Siege Warfare Volume II.* Routledge & Kegan Paul, London, 1985.

Duffy, C. *Fire and Stone: The Science of Fortress Warfare, 1660–1860.* Greenhill Books, London, 1996 (originally published 1975).

Gallacher, I. 'The Messines Mines, 1917', *Military Illustrated*, 37 (June 1991), 26–31.

Gille, B. *The Renaissance Engineers.* Lund Humphries, London, 1966.

Grant Grieve, Captain W., and Newman, B. *Tunnellers: The Story of the Tunnelling Companies, Royal Engineers, during the World War.* Naval & Military Press, Heathfield, 2001 (originally published 1936).

Gravett, C., Hook, R., and Hook, C. *Medieval Siege Warfare.* Osprey, London, 1990.

Greenshields, M.F. 'The Siege of Bedford Castle', *Bedfordshire Magazine,* volume 4 (1953), 183–90.

Harrington, P. *Archaeology of the English Civil War.* Shire, Princes Risborough, 1992.

Jones, S. 'Miners on the Western Front: Tunnelling Companies, Royal Engineers, 1915–17', *Military Illustrated*, 75 (August 1994), 36–39.

Kennedy, H. *Crusader Castles.* Cambridge University Press, 1994.

Kern, P.B. *Ancient Siege Warfare*. Indiana University Press, Bloomington, 1999.

Kightly, C. *Strongholds of the Realm. Defence in Britain from Prehistory to the Twentieth Century*. Thames & Hudson, London, 1979.

Lenihan, P. 'Aerial Photography: A Window on the Past', *History Ireland*, 2 (summer 1993), 9–13.

Mangold, T., and Penycate, J. *The Tunnels of Cu Chi*. Pan Books, London, 1986.

Marshall, C. *Warfare in the Latin East, 1192–1291*. Cambridge University Press, 1992.

Oman, C. *A History of the Art of War in the Middle Ages*. Two volumes. Methuen, London, 1924.

Oman, C. *A History of the Art of War in the Sixteenth Century*. Methuen, London, 1937.

Parker, G. *The Military Revolution*. Cambridge University Press, 1988.

Pepper, S. 'The Underground Siege', *Fort*, 10 (1982), 31–8.

Pepper, S., and Adams, N. *Firearms and Fortifications: Military Architecture and Siege Warfare in Sixteenth-Century Sienna*. University of Chicago Press, 1986.

Roberts, I. *Pontefract Castle*. West Yorkshire Archaeology Service, Wakefield, 1990.

Rogers, R. *Latin Siege Warfare in the Twelfth Century*. Oxford University Press, 1992.

Rothrock, G.A. (editor and translator). *A Manual of Siegecraft and Fortification by Sébastien Le Prestre de Vauban*. University of Michigan Press, Ann Arbor, 1968.

Sandes, Lieutenant-Colonel E.W.C. *The Military Engineer in India*. Institution of Royal Engineers, Chatham, 1933.

Seymour, W. *Great Sieges of History*. Brassey's, London, 1991.

Smith, C.S., and Gnudi, M.T. (editor and translator). *The Pirotechnia of Vannoccio Biringuccio*. MIT Press, Cambridge, Massachusetts, 1943.

Stoye, J. *The Siege of Vienna*. Birlinn, Edinburgh, 2000 (originally published 1964).

Turnbull, S. 'Taking Cyprus', *Military Illustrated*, 156 (May 2001), 48–55, 66.

Warner, P. *Sieges of the Middle Ages*. Bell, London, 1968.

Wiggins, K. *Anatomy of a Siege: King John's Castle, Limerick, 1642*. Wordwell, Bray, and Boydell Press, Woodbridge, 2000.

Wiggins, K., and Whyte, E. 'Something Worth Crowing About', *Archaeology Ireland*, 53 (autumn 2000), 30–33.

Yadin, Y. *The Art of War in Biblical Lands in the Light of Archaeological Discovery*. Weidenfeld & Nicolson, London, 1963.

Index